THE MERSEY GOLDFISH

THE MERSEY GOLDFISH

IAN DUHIG

BLOODAXE BOOKS

ISBN: 1 85224 325 2

First published 1995 by
Bloodaxe Books Ltd,
P.O. Box 1SN,
Newcastle upon Tyne NE99 1SN.

Bloodaxe Books Ltd acknowledges
the financial assistance of Northern Arts.

Cover printing by J. Thomson Colour Printers Ltd, Glasgow.

Printed in Great Britain by
Cromwell Press Ltd, Broughton Gifford, Melksham, Wiltshire.

In memory of my brothers
Adrian and Kevin

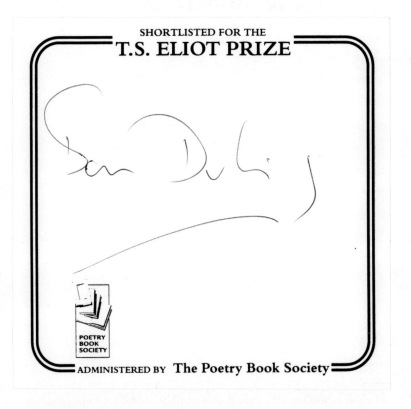

Acknowledgements

Acknowledgements are due to the editors of the following publications in which some of these poems first appeared: *Bête Noire, The Big Issues* (Dublin), *Blue Cage, Fortnight, Gown, The Guardian, The Honest Ulsterman, The Irish Review, New Statesman & Society, The New Yorker, North, Poetry Review, Poetry Wales, The Printer's Devil, Rhinoceros, Sheaf* and *The Wide Skirt.* 'The Gloss' also appears in *Northern Antiquity: The Post-Medieval Reception of Edda and Saga,* edited by A. Wawn.

A number of these poems were written for a commission from the Ilkley Festival in 1993 for a joint work with composer Christopher Fox. The result, *In the Key of H,* was first performed there in 1994.

I would particularly like to acknowledge the help of the Society of Authors, whose timely grant enabled me to finish this book.

Contents

The First Second

My young son claimed total recall from the sperm
    last bathnight, which stopped me like a clock.
From my immobilised hands he prised the oil
    that proofs his scalp against baptism
and turned right through me his orphanmaker-look,
    locking the continents of my skull
into jigsaws of his own. Then he could see

stars round my head from that crack on the lintel
    one fathom dead above the bald rug
outside my parent's cellar, hear my father's
    'Only Christ grew six foot to the nail!'
and Father Konstant's 'Imagine a steel egg
    bigger than the entire universe
brushed once every century by a dove's wing:
    when that whole egg is worn to nothing
is as the first second of eternity!'

Estuary English

During the hundredth birthday of James Joyce
while on the tiles of a WC
I mused upon Irish economy;
the language has sacked its K, Q and X
yet the meaning of whiskey's Kafkaesque;
in the cold bog of that Galway hotel
where all the world's newspapers are displayed
under glass like great ugly butterflies
I looked into my heart and my entrails
before the page of the *Wall Street Journal*
recording the poet Qin Guan's death
by drink – who forefathered the Shanghai God
before that economic journalist
overlooked the Q I made of myself.
On the green outside, *The Galway Hooker*
riffled with a squall off the Atlantic,
its sheet-steel rig heaving and quivering...
Somewhere a till gloated: *I Ching, I Ching*
like asdic basketing a submarine
then 'OK?' which was possibly 'O.Cé?'
asked the door of my palace of wisdom.
I brought up the Irish *abha* ('river'),
'ea', its lovely lost English sister,
name of Babylon's water deity,
then launched into my own flood-narrative.
The answer was Noah's, Utnapishtim's:
'Now tell me what you mean when you say *ark*?'

Fred

Not all that tempts one's wand'ring eyes
is fairly won as lawful prize,
   hinc illae lachrymae.
Fred burned his fairground booth red-gold,
my son, then I, then he were sold.
   Fred died the self-same day.

A few hours purpling our kitchen shelf...
kaput. I think he killed himself.
   I hid him from the son
I later told a dolphin stirred
to bear Fred's soul Fish-Asgardward,
   how royally he'd gone!

But no man wrote his epitaph;
with one flush of the cenotaph –
   transubstantiation.
A consummation to be wished,
Fred was the word made flesh made fish,
   Prince of Goldfish Nation.

My dreams ran red with Fred going west;
down The Cut, through Liverpool's est-
   uary (take a breath),
the Irish Sea's transgenic soup
boiling like a kaleidoscope
   half-life to life-in-death;

on to Dublin and to Galway
where swam ashore folk from Cathay,
   swore grey-eyed Columbus;
where fish circling St Brendan's Mass
bear Fred to the Americas,
   to survive in numbers.

Sampler Verses

From the Bottom of My Heart

My son forgets, so I remind him
as Dad nagged me so I'd wipe mine;
we contemplate, as Dads behind him,
skidmarks in the pants of time.

Mirror, Mirror

I just can't see why '96'
is better than straight coition,
but my wife tells me it's risqué
and her favourite position.

Summer

Summer: my bus up Chapeltown Road
passed an old man sat outside a pub,
legend under and on his t-shirt:
THE INCREDIBLY LARGE PENIS CLUB.

Snow

Sub Rosa

I rehearsed for the role of Job's comforter
on my sister, for her Confirmation Name,
Dympna, who was patron saint of the insane.
I would tell her she could be called Uncumber,
known as 'The Wilgefortis of Portugal'

(come to which she could be called Wilgefortis),
whose sole prayer was to end her life a virgin.
Through Christ she was 'uncumbered' of her suitors
by growing a beard and sideburns overnight.
The Prince of Sicily had her crucified.

In time I had my own secret moniker –
Monica's revenge for the Sack of Carthage.
Her son might be kissed by martyred virgins,
he might've had the *Cogito* prefigured
but he still had a name like an egg in a beard.

Brut

(after Sir Frederic Madden's Poetical Semi-saxon Paraphrase
of the Cottonion and related British Museum manuscripts)

For horned Menelaus
the Greeks took Old Troy,
salted its vineyards,
slaughtered its folk,
poor innocent bastards
reduced all to words,
a right bloody stroke
from his friends and relations,
their oars in for Helen –
O praise for her boat-race
surpasses my art,
but you'd fork out a fiver
just to hear the girl fart.
So when the old king
tired of twanging his string
he called in all favours,
suggested a raid
to make them all famous:
Siege of the Decade!
The price on the meter?
Think of a number,
say: all those you've met.
Think of them dead.
You've got the picture.
Troy got the point.
Some people blame her
who never raised sword,
others the dick-thing
men get about war.
And that woody horse?
Boxed half a batalion?
Some sex-toy it was,
no I-talian stallion.

In Greek propaganda
Old Trojans believe
the slaver Cassandra
serves from tea leaves,
but she thought the beast
was breed of the breed of
Catherine the Great's
traction contraption,
who felt the best Ovid
translates best to action.

A Repeat

This episode of *Sesame Street* is brought to you
by the letter *K.K.* Picture it metamorphose:
the angle of a mannekin's shocking pink knee;
its off-the-shoulder gathered like a kilt
at the hip; the shop-window itself, half-
curtained to effect kitchen intimacy.

Knock the glass. Faces echo back in galleries
like a tunnel; the S-bahn; the S-bahn trains surfed
by drum-headed men; the watchfulness of dark rose-sellers.
I call you through the valley of the shadow of our hotel,
its breakfast sausage more various than snowflakes,
china hens with cold, soft eggs and post-mortem lavatories.

Knock again. Daylight steadies into our reflections
on the thick glass door a clothes-shop owner in Berlin
locks twice: in your face as lovely as a rose-sellers',
in mine the second time for realising this. Think
how the key scrabbles first like *kuklos*, then like *klan*,
how the owner's eyes leave silver trails on their sealed tank.

A chip of quartz somewhere replays a day well-spent
feasting in the owner's face on next-door's superb pies;
forest-fruits lapped by strawberry aces, that Kirsch glaze
that still comes over me when I remember them;
the baker's lady who sold them and her open smile.
Mark these with *K*. Repeat: even the burps taste magnificent.

1992

Europe's invasion of America
but also softer anniversaries –
a century since that Welsh auction
of the *Santa Maria's* genuine log,
its historical importance obvious
with the entries all in the Queen's English.

Like Colón, Columba wrote prophecies –
he forecast the discovery of 'Ind'
and errata of novice copyists
(he saw one vowel awol from its psalter
rise like Nelson above O'Connell Street,
illuminating the capital of Ireland).

Columba caused the Battle of the Books
with his unauthorised reproduction
of passages from St Finian's Psalter,
spied at night through his anachronistic
keyhole by one of St Finian's monks
working to light that poured from his fingers.

Could it grow cucumbers or cauliflowers?
Clarify Brendan's geography?
Why Colón should write his log in English
not Welsh? A thirst was sharpened in the monk
until the beak of Columba's pet crane
filled the keyhole with its signifier.

Lost Boys

The day from the big burn he hooked a trout
that would pull the scales through seven pound
(to train the wee stuttering rhetorician
he'd slipped into its little mouth a stone),
when he'd turned away to tie his special fly,
in case, he said, smaller fish should snatch it;
the day he'd cut back to watch out for by the jetty

osmundroyal, marsh pennywort, water bedstraw,
the asphodel and the bog-myrtle – which was itself,
men leant back to quote, 'a beautiful emblem of the
Christian: who needs be pounded in affliction's mortar
before the odour of his grace will flow out in words',
the words flowing from the most unpounded of them,
their eyes still shining with that familiar old light;

the day, to try to get back to the beginning,
he got back to wailing, a short coffin on big As,
trestles shining with their blackwash coats still wet
and Davy, cold as pence. This is the beginning. He
climbed to the dark room where his mother cried his name,
O vain tabernacle, his mother cried the name of her Davy.
After her breath ran out he breathed 'it's no him, only me'.

He wrote 'the pretty boy glides like a ray of black sunshine'.
He put away egg-cap, put away even the capey-dykey.
His wife asked him to stop kissing her goodnight
as a gift for their Tin Wedding Anniversary.
He's the one we call The Boy Who Couldn't Get Up.
He knew too much dead babies will not teach us,
and the words. But don't worry. It's no him, only me.

A Lorca Gacela

The dead feather themselves with moss.
The clouded wind and the clear wind
are game birds whirring between towers
and the day is an injured child.

Afternoons, the water gets sat down
with its pals, has a bit of a laugh.
Where I come from such afternoons,
each such afternoon costs a child's life.

Not a wisp of cloud stuck to the sky
when we met in the caves of wine;
no tuft of cloud snagged on a thorn
when you became taken by water.

A monster of water broke on the fells
and the dogs rolled and the lilies rolled;
under my violet-shadowed hands
you were an archangel of cold.

Note

I earned my number in King Chocolate's gold city
   the Easter their Mysteries needed a page
for a float playing baroque meditational lyrics.
   With my nose-flute I inhaled arpeggios
of H and cocaine while the rest practised parading.
   Then one day I sneezed on stage: the whole *tableaux*
was really *vivant* with the snuff that dreams are made on.

The next day five boys from the Festival Committee
   touched me with an offer I couldn't refuse,
the chance of a new position. It was missionary
   (*toque delicado que la vida*
eterna sabe y toda deuda paga),
   not as hard as the conversion of the Jews;
remote, but the word was leprosy was dropping off.

It was the Atlantic, not the Pacific Ocean
   fat Cortés spied from his peak at Darien,
but with my belly-bilge in perpetual motion
   they could have landed me at any verse-end.
After I had vomited up my final toenail
   I met my Boss, the bishop of my new home,
the most leprous island of its archipelago

but with a flora pleasurably abusable.
   The bishop outlined his plan for an airstrip
serviced by lepers harvesting and packing the crop;
   the company logo for his new firm, 'Hy Brasil'.
He swore we could turn over new leaves and a profit
   till, Dear Reader, I finally strangled him
and his tongue lolled onto the sand like a flesh bass clef.

Every day, tides sweep these beaches like a surplice.
   The skies are violet as a child's veins
or flecked with manna. They breathe with absolute silence.
   The island lies under a dome of goodwill
while offshore interest is in the gift of dolphins
   tearing their element like blue violins.
This is my testament. Replace it in its bottle.

Ten Desert Island Books

The Joy of Sex On Your Own

An t-Oileánach (trans. Brian O'Nolan)

St Brendan the Voyager: His Shipwright's Manual

Uses and Abuses of the Banana

So You Think You Know About Sand?

Appelation Controlée Palm Wine; How To Make It. Market It and Get Rich While Marooned

Psychotropic Flora of the Pacific

Nuclear War: A Good Scoff at 'The Developed World'

O'Neill's 1001 Tunes Adapted for the Conch

The Wisdom of Turtles

Realm of the Coin

Cobwebs in his purse, Arrius's 'h's,
horribile aequor ultimosque
Britannos, where the earth takes enemas,
stirred Catullus's interest, but Caesar?

He didn't know the colour of his skin,
he claimed (a technique perfected by Wilde –
the culturedly ignorant question),
though he knew that all Caesars' skins are gold.

Sunk into a tray of well-mown velvet,
Offa looks strikingly like a Caesar,
or the heads they chose to represent themselves.
His moneyers borrowed from the *dinar* –

the 'Celtic pattern' a ringing Kufic
MUHAMMAD IS THE PROPHET OF ALLAH.
The owner knows this but will not have it.
He can quote its value to the dollar.

Second Hand

I heard it on the radio;
  the brazen harpsichord
and Ó Riada (*née* Reidy)
  firing jacks at Arp's words,

his poem 'Sekundenzeiger'
  I know as 'Second Hand',
with thanks to Michael Hamburger,
  Leeds Market Bookstall and

its unappreciative staff.
  Also, for 30p,
a famous art-collector's Life,
  quite priceless on Arp's youth –

the Arp of Tzara, pal of Ball
  his German first name shed:
'Hans' no longer unpaid his bills
  a 'Jean' dodged them instead.

You could say No Go Beethoven
  was Arp's post-war politics;
German music was *verboten,*
  he'd just shout 'Candlesticks!'

(his sum of English) 'Candlesticks'
  He roared it all the time,
which didn't seem to damp the wick
  of Peggy Guggenheim.

English, German, *tickt und tackt sie,*
  we clock up no extras
when we catch the last black taxi
  and our real name is brass.

The Gift of a Black Egg

In my left hand, Uasal Ní Dhomhnaill,
nests your gift of a polished basalt egg
as smooth as the *ubh* and *dubh* in Duhig.
Heaney used one for the ball of a heel
of the Grauballe man, a bog sacrifice.
Chinese women sewed them into their clothes –
a flick of the wrists made coshes of sleeves.
My mother's tongue fell on my neck the night
I drilled verbs after a Gaelic League class.
She taught me 'kibosh' is an Irish word,
sentence commuted if I'd just shut up.
I write 'thank you' and '*go raibh maith agat*',
try to speak. I can't. I wet my lips
and a black bird flies out of my mouth.

Traditional

My uncle measures me aged one:
'arse-high to a magpie's gallus-button!'

The day I married I watched two
threaten the stitching of their shiny suits

like the drunks at our wedding-dance.
I noticed the first time at my third glance

between the shoulders of those suits
a hint of a glint of gunmetal blue;

tails held with waiterly aplomb
splashing the colours of a petrol-bomb;

the mercury tilt to their eyes.
Four of them mean birth. A dearth comes with five;

noisy families thick as thieves
augurs and understood relations have

by maggot-pies and choughs and rooks
the skewbald is familiar with six.

Seven babes buried in the dark.
Blood-libel birds, murderers from the ark.

The *Noli Me Tangere* Tango

She was disguised when I met her at the broo,
so she could sign on for her twin sister.
I know. I asked her about that too:
'Who do you imagine would've missed her?'

She hissed her sister was off on a course.
I asked, of course, and she answered 'signing'!
'Couldn't she make a thumbprint or a cross?'
'No not *signing*, you idiot, SIGNING!'

Her own fingers flew in a translation.
If she had long nails they would've scarred her.
Pictures boomed in my imagination;
Sooty, naked, dancing the lambada

and Simon's friend at her new school. First day
(with friendly faces just a wee bit scant)
she gets told her SIGNING's the giveaway –
it's just so obviously Protestant.

You can dance flamenco solo
as you can the gay fandango,
some can even can-can one-man
O but it takes two to tango,
to tango it takes two. Thank you.

The Christmas Fairy

It wasn't the Christmas Fairy I caught by the presents
but Inspector Berkshire taking a footprint from my sock.
He turned, speaking of his Burke family connections,
which he shares with Her Majesty, while pocketing the clock.
He asked for my signature on a string of petitions,
blank as then, for campaigns to preserve Habeas Corpus.

He gingered his whiskey before drafting my confession
and bubbles in golden chains flowed from my victim's body
when she broke through the ice, glittering like the morning star
but lashed like some martyred Tinker Bell to my Christmas tree.
He felt for a tissue while his pocket struck the New Year,
priming my WELCOME mat for the print of the first left foot.

The Protestant's Dog-Thieves

The first night of the twelve nights of Christmas
my father's wren boys, rumoured to behave worse
than the Algerian pirates in Baltimore,
painted Guard Dwyer's cottage orange while he snored,
wrapped Snout, his Pekinese, in a horse-blanket
and escaped to imperial blasts on the trombone
they'd stolen from him when he marched with the Blueshirts.

As midnight mass muttered its Confiteors
Snout, inwardly pure from his soapy enema,
skittered toward the altar till Mrs Connors
stunned him with her missal. Christ's anathema
was called on the Protestant's Dog-Thieves in Latin
by the same Canon Walsh who called bingo numbers
in Latin so Guard Dwyer's wife couldn't win.

If

If you can calculate the last three figures
of tomorrow's total dollar sales volume
at the closure of the New York Stock Exchange
from dreambooks of a jackleg evangelist
who is upright but unconscious in the john
of the brownstone firetrap you are both squatting
while one brother cooks his hair with lye and screams
another is profiling the punjab pants
that cut off the blood to your feet in Roseland
and your eyes are chapel hatpegs from the dope,
you have correctly interpreted this dream:

you're skating backwards at the Palomar Rink
from the note in the Mr Goodbar wrapper
she's carefully pincering with a mitten
bonded umbilically to its sister
by three inches short of enough elastic
threading both sleeves of both her knitted waistcoats
so she just drifts, stiffer than John Henry's ghost,
her arms wide as if in African prayer,
her outline fuzzing with your myopia,
her face already lost with the expression
which might mean 'LuvU2' or 'Where's the candy?'

Ex Libris

If all God's chillun got their chance on wings
what a coming home to roost there would be;
if the joyful burst their clouds like pillows
smart cuckoos would be huddling at the bar.

Some Jim Harris then, some Malcolm Little
might unslub a gloss from The Moor's fortunes,
the incontinence of his self-slaughter,
the scholarship built upon a tissue.

He might, like Malcolm, unmask Shakespeare as
Na Caca Père, King James VI and I;
The Moor as Omar and therefore Homer.
A woman might serve us with the same sauce –

for men, in the words of Emilia,
'… eat us hungerly, and when they are full,
They belch us.' If she bit into this poem
music would escape. Then a Jim Crow smell.

Gyron's Submission

Sire, I am no soothsayer – to say other
would be economical with the sooth,
but I have glimpsed the future, and it's rough
if you let Boggerlas play Oedipus.
Forget the sledded Polacks and turn west
to its Ultima Thule, Britannia,
which is begging for your paternosters.
You've a claim that's etymological
and letters congruing to that effect:
two *U*s there means you're doubly upper-class.
B stands for Bacon, author of Shakespeare
and the pig's nest of your family tree.
Airt Uí Laoghaire's like Arturo Ui
and remember *I* once meant Iona,
while you've loved Wales since reading *Moby Dick*.
Your *roi* was fetched by *rex* from Dog Latin,
like the *rí* in the Irish *Rí*public.
MacRitchie's 'Ancient and Modern Britons'
finds *roi* in both aboriginal tribes
of archipelagical indigenes:
Melanochroi Africal colonists
and Celtic-Anglo-Saxon *Xanthochroi*,
perfidious albino parodies
escaped from Yacub's laboratories –
'... but the traces of our black ancestry'
I quote verbatim from its first volume
'are existent in a hundred surnames' –
MacRitchie cites Dooley, Douglas, Duffy,
sifting earth from their roots in Gaelic *dubh*.
How I envy you this royal foray
and tragedy it is I must remain
but you'd never get me past their Customs Men:
they would take me for the wrong sort of black.

Die Schwarze Paula

You debauched our currency, sowed our wells
with cholera, defiled our history
not because you are a victor nation
but because you are a victim nation:
you are a Jew or you work for a Jew
who knows all wars and no wars are civil.

The stars pass like a torchlight procession
in Alexandria where I was born,
the full moon is a dish of rotten figs
or fouled light in a judas-hole.
Some of me will be forever Alexandrine.
You English would hate it, you'd hate the 'wogs'.

I loved his silences on the platform
when he would pose, hands cupped over his groin.
The last pet-name he gave me was *Dickkopf* –
better than *Schwarze Paula* or *Fräulein*
(Jews spread word I painted my toenails red).
Then I was *Z*, and where I lived *Camp Z*.

I met *C*, an *M'*, the *W Board*,
the *Y Service*, the *XX Committee*
sometimes called *The Twenty* but well I know
was Masterman's Double-Cross Committee –
according to his quack I must possess
'a mind as virginal as Robespierre's'.

I think I used to fake the amnesia.
I am sure that this camp's name is Spandau,
its guards Marx's 'backward Asiatics'.
Half the world thinks I am an imposter.
The mask I wear is, I think, my real skin.
It is my will that's iron, not my face.

Unity

'A harlot's pistol she shot herself with –
very small calibre – your Lady Macbeth.'
The Count's English hissed like his silk slacks.
'She had to learn to speak and write again
and she had to wear nappies, she could not...'
his gesture, a delicate arabesque.
So perfect was its execution
it could have been his signature in the air,
stopping as his pen ran out of music.
'I received a pitiful letter from her...'
gold-framed sunglasses slid like a visor
from a helmet still golden to its roots
'perhaps I should feel ashamed of myself...'
a moon also hung over the dark forest,
pierced like an Ernst. My last tape flapped.
An ancient servant drove me into town:
'the Leader said you English girls have flesh
like peaches from the rains, your English rains?'
I said in Egland it had never rained.
He smiled: 'She slept with the entire SS.'

*

Her Muv thumped crocquet hoops into the lawn
around Farve, flapping on his shooting-stick
complaining *The Times* hadn't been ironed
(a sharp gust had carried off the prices) –
he'd glanced above the obituaries
at windows sunk like traps in his ivied wall
and lost both pages when he glimpsed his daughter
feigning strangulation with a sash-cord.
Her owlish cheek was crushed against the pane.
Farve, n. (irreg.), *uuge and objegzionable* –
she defined him in her argot;
'My language had to go with a facial
expression which was one of great sorrow
words escaping from the side of one's mouth.'

She cursed her family with *gommid id*,
the *id* to *gommid* being suicide.
The buttergold tongue of an angel
was hard as a gun behind her virgin teeth.

*

The girl will make a record in a booth
like Pinky out of *Brighton Rock*: 'duYIDZ duYIDZ
wiGUDDuh gedRIDDuh DUH YIDZ.' The girl
became a woman always wearing black.
She fell in love with a man who wore black.
Yesterday, she came home with his peace terms
and a Christian wound in her temple
from her anguish in the *Englischer Garten*.
Her swelling progress will take in Scotland,
faces slipping like rain through her fingers.
She will be carried to 'Columskill'
like a king in Shakespeare or a fairy tale.
She will recall her lover's favourite song,
a huntsman weeps for his girl by moonlight.
Her small calibre moon will weep and night
circle like a disc on a gramophone.

Nightsoil

What did you do in the War then Daddy?
Mine wisely defended neutrality
while his in '16, an armchair Fenian
could see demonstrated the theorem
which states that Irish opportunities
haemorrhage from English difficulties.
One night, covering a hostel alone
I booked in a hero fit for a home,
wheezing like the hinge on the hostel gate
he looked a man cut away from the stake;
toothless – he'd've given them more easily
than details of his personal history.
I grew brutal in my questioning
when he kept bringing up 1916 –
all flows from this *Annus Mirabilis*.
Over charlock, poppy and scabious,
machine-guns closing their butterfly wings
and artillery coughing up its lungs
as silently as any butterfly;
silently he watches while silently
bullets twitch in the grass like grasshoppers,
twitches the German snipers' periscopes;
now he sees schoolfriends falling like cornstalks,
now and always he sees his schoolfriends fall
making no more sound than the falling night,
that one, the only one he would stay for.
I am told one man is a warrior
so that his son can become a farmer,
so that his son can become a poet.
Good. I can stay ignorant or forget
the crude measure they danced in the Somme mud
clumsily, stupid as calves smelling blood.

Come the Morning

(AIR: *The Trees They Do Grow High*)

As the trees lose all their leaves
evenings close round me
and I think on all the dreams that's passed
since my young man I seen,
now I must make my bed in the crook of this blind lane
with a bonny boy who's young, but who's growing.

At the age of 15 years
with him I fell in love,
the morning of his 16th year
I delivered him a son;
before my man was 17
on his grave the grass grew green –
pure heroin buried him, now he's growing.

They brought my love a shroud
of the oriental brown,
for each needle's stitch I found in it
O a tear it did run down;
who once I kissed so hungrily
kissed the night below –
not his own flesh and blood, nor sees him growing.

They came to take my baby
in the middle of the night,
'It's for the best' one bastard said
and I'm sure that she was right.
O I'd never walk these streets alone
now I walk these streets alone.
I've forgotten all your names come the morning.

(Repeat first verse).

B I Ballad

When He put a(n) *h* into Abraham
there wasn't a run on Dumbarton spam
but folk niggled when they should've begat –
say it this way you must, you must say that –

till all they could get up was objections.
Hence Tamar-Tephi's flight with Jacob's Stone,
your genuine Ark of the Covenant
and royal matchmakers to County Ant-

rim. Our Princess married an Irish king,
Elizabeth II descending;
the Ark stopped at Tara, the Stone took in
'Saint Colme's Inch', anchoring in London.

So there we are: not some wandering Jews
but British and Israelite and kosher;
His imperial tribe by Him chosen
to rule and stave off thin ends of wedges.

Cosby's Noah couldn't know 'a cubit':
our number's prime Egyptology mensch
proved The Great Pyramid of Giza built
'to the forerunner of the British inch.'

These inches, feet, measured Jerusalem
in His blue Jacobean-English tongue:
bang on the *M* of the Millenium
we'll hear His trump and here we'll come again!

The Soothsayer

One time when Caesar bled in sport
as Soothsayer, the script forgot
I cried 'All right! What is't a clock
doing in Imperial Rome?'
I had half-hoped that Miss O'Rourke
would lose her rag and send me home

but no; she smiled and sweetly said
another word I'd see The Head.
A Cinna so I tried once more
to effect a greater schism,
'Miss O'Rourke! I understand now!
Shakespeare's using *anarchism!*'

In my son's school the clocks are quartz
with *3*s and *6*s, *9*s and *O*s.
Outside my Headmaster's office
the huge clock used *X*s, *I*s and *V*s.
It spelt out Latin certainly.
Dreams strayed over its Roman face.

Roll Call

He prints SAM JACKS on the mailman's form,
takes the packets of galleys, gets thanked
as 'Mr Trumbo' and fled from.
Back inside, he refills his coffee-flasks:

both his heads are on this writer's block.
90% of the script might work –
plot and character are well-defined –
but it's the end. He can see no end,

no gesture enacting its testament.
Has he come to the well too often?
What was it again that *testa* meant?
Jug. Pot. Slang for a man's head, cut off,

ears for handles, rolling in its own wine.
That's IT or he's ISN'T Sam Trumbo:
the last stand of the slave rebellion
crushed by the force of sheer Roman numbers;

a rump at the mercy of Crassus.
He crows 'Give him up and save your lives!'
Silence. Focus on Kirk's heroic face.
The mike strains for his 'I am Spartacus'

but his neighbour roars in stereo
'HE LIES. I, I AM SPARTACUS',
then the next man's 'IT IS I' and the next:
'I', 'I', 'I', 'I', 'I AM SPARTACUS.'

Sam Goldfish

Courts had to get the -*fish* out of my name.
Selwyn claimed I stole his last syllable,
Mayer that my *G* was owned by MGM.
They were laughed out as im and possible.

Some words were mine. H-bombs are dynamite.
I praised Churchill's 'great poisonality'.
I will never forget his face that night.
He said '(DELETE) jew', very quietly.

Malatesta

His form-master wrote him off as giftless,
so he wheeled in smoked hams, farm parmesans,
trays of the priestchoker local pasta:
but after he sported up to Prize Day
in The Party black *Sahariana*
even the Head declared himself impressed.
Indulgences became his penances
and no bird sounded like his school reports.

Every Latin class of his last year
he scratched the surface of thick laundry ink
the Head ruled in the School 'Satyricon'.
One replacement Teacher of History
told him Abyssinia's Holy Rose
and the Elephant of Mnemosyne
featured on Malatesta's coat of arms
(but not what the name meant, where it came from).

By the *Tempio Malatestina*
the graduate sold his caricatures
till *Il Duce*'s ban. *Fotoromanzi*
next killed his back-up trade in silhouettes;
cut to Visconti, 'Red Duke of Milan';
he drinks *grappa*, ridicules film-makers
whose surnames trail into peasant *-inis*,
who boast of cartwheels on their family crests.

Old Shanghai

English prints of the film *Kagemusha*
lack one character, Uesegi Kenshin
who was smitten at his lavatory
and dead in three days. Our source blamed a worm,
inscribing so in the court diary.
Unluckily, his master was struck dumb;

the royal tissue is still at question.
Doctors now vote cancer or go for stroke.
Others believe the warlord was with child
or the subject of assassination.
My name is Uubike. Only I know.
First let me take you back to Old Shanghai,

then we'll journey by ninja submarine
to the mountains and pray for Founder En.
We'll swallow our shadows like the moat carp
and climb Castle Kenshin's walls in salt-crusts
to the level of a room he enters
for the last time. He draws the paper screen.

It frames a poem written in white ink
as a subliminal ideogram
explaining the thesis of *Repression*:
IDEALS DEVELOP FROM THEIR OPPOSITES!
The calligraphic 'voice' seems familiar,
fluent, yet draining a glass of black milk

you're spluttering all down your kimono,
the new kimono you're growing into.
The spilled milk dries to a white silhouette
on the cutting-room floor. You are guilty
and being hanged by your own narrative thread
Uubike, my old china. Sign below.

Untitled

*Out of these enmities, indeed, would come a new efflorescence
*– especially of poetry in the work of Seamus Heaney, Michael
Longley, Derek Mahon and Patrick Muldoon.*

       F.S.L. LYONS,
       Culture and Anarchy in Ireland

No Derry slubberdegullion with college airs,
no mushroom visions in Wexford sheds (well, not *Wexford*),
no continuing city father with gentle breasts
and high voice since his run-in with the barber's missus –
no: you were the quietest. You were surely the best:

Running Over Toads on the Ballygawley Roundabout;
Squeezing the Brains out of Toads – each an epiphany.
Your assurance crumbled after your quoof escaped,
excluding yourself from your own anthology
(but nearly everybody else into the bargain),

finally you lost even what you stood up in
to some imposter from a parallel universe
(the Moy). He painted spectacles over your face
in all your photographs, insinuated himself
into your fingerprints and remodelled your signature.

To this very day I remain flabbergasted
that folks could be suckered by such a flagrant hoax,
and I've a flabber not gasted by a trifle,
'Paul'! Sounds Mick to me. Now 'Patrick' from the Old Norse
Pad-rekr, at least that means something: 'Exiler of Toads'.

Double Vision,
or A Second Sight at *Second Sight*

My father's mother had trouble with geography –
Flanders began at the kitchen window –
that sort of thing. Gas was blamed
for turning antimacassars yellow
when the wind blew in from the privy.

Crossing the water to visit her
I have brought the *Pocket Guide to London*,
my *Map of the Underground*, Keble-Martin's
Concise British Flora in Colour,
Old Moore's Almanac, *The Tibetan Book of the Dead*,

a compass, a sextant, powerful
binoculars of German manufacture,
a very large ball of cobbler's thread,
fourteen bottles of Jamesons
and some valium to help me find her.

Where is my father's house, where my father?
Where *is* Clapham Common? If I could only find
my grandmother's place I'd walk straight in –
she'd see right through me and the hallway, past
the ball of thread uncoiling from Belfast

and cry, 'Who the bloody hell are you?'

The Exhibition

I was voted 'cultural outrider'
for my Neo-Situationist cadre
on a day I hardly remember,
(the homebrew, the lump of red leb).

To expose the Bridget Riley show
I wore 3-D glasses from a *Freddy* film
(the one with most Roman numerals).
Up close to one I became an imbroglio,

poleaxed by my new angle on Op Art.
The deck hit me, put my crown through my top lip
and sank a red kiss into its carpet.
As I said to the guard, thith wath 'Thpectacle',

the key Neo-Thituationitht conthept.
He told me he sympathised with my view;
he knew nothing about art, but he too
could make an exhibition of himself.

Portrait of the Artist

Kings Cross then; a child's shoddy gaberdine
fits him like the clapper fits our school bell.
He strokes the nap of my herringbone tweed,
flicks a button as if it's a football

and says a doorknob gave him the black eye.
Our labels tangle. Mine's furrowed in wax
by the nice name for Aunt Sweaty Betty,
who meant food, cold or photograph by *snap*.

No game. My skylight had blanket curtains.
Six forks supported greasy lengths of felt
until Joe Keuys fixed me up with shutters,
like on a cuckoo-clock. The day he left

late frost hid in the shadows of her trees.
He smiled over a row of word-balloons –
finishing the silverware at Betty's
he smiled like that at her, across the spoons.

Portrait of the Art

I

Art stuffs. This Job Description is half Jarry's.
Sure enough, performances of *Ubu Rex*,
he claimed, need 'Saveloys' in their orchestras
while M'Nure splits nave to chops 'like a sausage.'

II

My teeth left a crescent moon in my last slice,
in Bologna called *il grassa*, or 'the fat'.
She'd told me locally the part of the ass
not pounded up for sausages was its fart.

III

I owe a man I don't know for all these words,
'Double Jobby' Bobby of Clydeside renown;
employed solely to sweep up shipyard cat turds
he didn't let the piece-rate grind him down.

One day, considering how his pay was spent,
he thought of the 'pschitt-scissors' of Père Ubu,
like as not, halved his next turd, claimed it as two –
and his bonus rose by one hundred per cent.

Images of Spit

The William

Your white william is valueless
for protocols of school insult:
its pristine unadhesive sud
is a face-slap with a lace glove.

The Gilbert

The solid gold yolk of a fresh egg
stands as proud as sunrise on its plate:
a hawked heart of emerald gilbert
clumps like shamrock on its victim's mug.

The Boris

The flob this bodies forth is serious:
kettle-cheeks of putti or seraphim
best mash its thick, tobacco-y mucous.
First class at distance. The cream of the phlegm.

Culchie Gough

The woollen snowflakes glued to our classroom window
crisp in the Easter sun over Juniors Playground.
Agnus Dei qui tollis peccata mundi
I mime, barred from the open air mass with my friend,
Culchie Gough. We had caffled at the Introit,
unfortunately within the teacher's earshot

who still frowns up at us, if sheepishly. The Pope
knighted him last week (*Domine non sum dignus*) –
'Order of the Creeping Jesus' Culchie hoped.
I decide to later beat up the altar boy.
His backlit ears shine like the hosts of honesty
peeling from bottled sticks on our nature table.

Pax Domini sit semper vobiscum. I hold
one pod, picturing a lobe, and the veins delta
like Culchie's gilbert on the inflatable world.
Green fingers stream from its North Pole to its Gobi
while I fog the windowpane with my coarse salute:
fgcoff! Eclipsis. He still laughs, is still dead. Goodbye.

Opus Dei

I

The wireless once said 'television' was a bastard word.
I scoffed on the Q.T. I could pronounce it easily
and loved the fact it had been invented by Yogi Bear.
Ours was a goldfish-bowl set in a double-wardrobe –
both shared the grain of pound notes. It had its own sabbath day,
when my family massed like an amphitheatre mob.
Darkly, the quiz-inquisitor in a forces blazer
ensnared greedy contestants with his Socratic Method,
his yes-no questions, into being damned in black and white
as a gongadier hunkered and the organist hovered:
a one-word answer and all was lost. For those who survived
life was a key of fivers climbing like the organ chords.
The whole world took sides: 'TAKE THE MONEY' or 'OPEN
          THE BOX!'

II

From deep inside his black habit, Father Bourque fished two keys
and silence brought up the maplewood smell of his chapel.
The first, its brass wings pierced like a stigmatic butterfly,
he settled on the square peg inside his box's round hole,
twisting until it creaked like hide then beat like a heart.
With the second he unlocked the minute wooden door,
lifting an ormolu monstrance onto the altarcloth.
It squatted like a Japanese knight in full battledress,
called an English word for shit eleven times, fell over
and stopped. As Hobbes was rising to prove he'd squared the circle
the oldest man in the tribe stood and turned to his people.
His people looked up at him like the Oxford professors.
He surveyed them for a very long time then fell over.
No one seemed to mind. They were going down with something else.

III

Not everyone knows how I killed Myles na gCopaleen,
sucking his heart out through the meniscus of his whiskey.
He saw me once in a glass, licking his cherubic lips,
but he took me to be himself. Truth is an odd number
according to Pythagoras, according to Plato.
I used to write confessions on the head of Fox's stout
(he's the character in charge of this investigation);
drained, an O dangled on his nose like an empty keyring,
the ridge of froth was like a sheepskin band on a racehorse.
Soon, C fell fast as the eclipsis in the genitive
from the 'name' under his newspaper column, *Cruiskeen Lawn!*
Prostituted to the Anglo-Saxon Epiglottis.
His piss-take salute took off our Lord Mayor's broken clock.
I gave him a broken clock to worry about OK.

The Medicine Rite

As long as the earth shall last, so long shall I make use of thee.
JOHN RAVE

John Rave was a bad Winnebago,
too poor for The Medicine Rite,
who made his way by peyote
to Christ in His cassock of night.

The Jesuits called John *mon brave*
and welcomed him into their Mission –
they hold to the grave souls like John Rave
for half the expense of a shaman.

John poured out his soul in Confession.
A blackrobe poured scotch in his tea,
mentioned the strings to absolution
before sinners can call themselves free.

Back in his wilderness John preached
the Winnebago must be reborn.
His John the Baptist never cheered
as much as his John Barleycorn.

From The Land of *Uz*

Grace drew me westward from the land of *Uz*
to dream a pharaoh's daughter at the *Cúirt*
say Ireland shared names with the wife of Job.
To check her facts I would set sail from Cobh,
my ark a basketwork of ivy leaves
and its belly proofed with the inky pitch.

The craft fetched north to the land of Israel,
a cassie halving the Egyptian seas –
I was hardly wiser than a salmon
fat from the nine hazels of poetry
when fire burned the skirt of a police jeep
in the Street of the Field of Ten Hazels.

Some charioteers smitten hip and thigh
by *Israel's* champions of their shared queen
were ringed by comrades in their injury.
A host of Israel's loyal womenfolk
climbed walls to look down on the broken men
offering such comfort: the men's beauty

would once have took the eye out of your head;
that they looked well among the tar and ash
since that each of them was a black bastard.
Later, champions triumphed in dark cars,
thumping horns in the first bars of *The Sash*
which the squaddies heard as 'sod' in Morse Code.

For Your Eyes Only

He was capable of statesmanlike behaviour
on occasion and a gallows sense of humour.
We voted him the Golden Shield for that first speech,
agreeing to hear it reread every year.
There was talk of naming a month in his honour
till his illness, the spate of enforced suicides,
his young bride divorced and banished in a fortnight,
the death sentence on a man who sold hot water.
His next wife was ugly but impossibly rich,
which seemed to contradict the theory he'd gone mad
till the deification of his 'close' sister
followed immediately thereon by his own.
Demanding sacrifices to his genius
we voted him a statue cast from solid gold –
instructing the sculptors not to rush their commission
when he announced he'd raise it in Jerusalem.
The actors stoked up his antisemitism,
besides the interest in wearing women's clothes.
The conspiracies abounded – to hear some now
you'd almost fill a circus with his murderers.
The rabble wept; they'd loved the games and public works
and he'd been popular with the equestrians.
Some of our class rioted with the commoners.
His bodyguard (with some disgust) restored order
though the succession is not settled as I write.
I wouldn't exactly say that we deserved him,
but one can't have chidren and remain a virgin.
We'll be less ambitious with our next candidate.

A Basket of Dalmatian Oysters

(i.m. Hubert Butler)

I

When I visited him in his office
I saw on his desk what I took to be
a basket of shelled Dalmatian oysters.
'A gift from my Bosnian Ustashe,'
he smiled. I looked closer and they were eyes.

II

You drink with them carafes of rakkia
and look for the forgiving among folk
in black for the Battle of Kosovo,
1389, year of the young Turk.
Like us, they ask about America.

And in the Depth

It is hard to be sure what prompted the Reverend George
William Garrett to desert the duties of his Manchester
curacy and enter the submarine business.

COMMANDER B.R. COMPTON-HALL, R.N., M.B.E.

Three years before *Leviathan* sank Hobbes,
An Ark for Submarine Navigation
propelled John Wilkins to his bishopric,
marriage with Oliver Cromwell's sister,
a place in the Royal Society.
His design for mechanical bowels

still evacuates navies round the world.
He was a challenge and inspiration
to Commander Garrett, B.A., Pasha.
His first *Resurgam* sprang a leak off Wales
and he cursed the ex-Christian Brother
with all O'Donovan Rossa's dollars.

Garrett turned to Mecca for new angels;
he preached by the waters of Babylon
of the Lamm Engine in his Behemoth;
in 'the Arabic poetry of Job'
he did not conceal its parts nor its power,
nor its comely proportion. I saw him

flicker at the bottom of my beerglass,
lost below the waist to his steel pulpit.
Flagless, his signals are a clock's mad prayer;
eight-fifty, eleven-ten, a quarter
past nine, six-fifteen, eight-thirty...
                                        ...long pause.
It seems he's forgotten the time for 'H'.

Six More Sides to the Muck Island Box

Eden has no biblical connotations.

DIXON DONALDSON,
History of Islandmagee

I *The Proverb*

Geographies unfurled
when the islandman said to me
'If you would go out of the world
go to Islandmagee.'

II *The Road to the Box*

'CHRIST 6ls th2 64rd thlt splk2 3t' –
the Ballycarry Croppy's epitaph
rises with the weather from the stone tongue
of bliss. It's as if words failed him; as if
he was mistrusting his way into song –
'HE t44k th2 64rd lnd brlk2 3t'

III *The Blah Hole, Whitehead*

At the lip of the Blah Hole
new light made words visible

in cold. You drove a stake through
the heart of my folk-myth,

that Shakespeare translated some Job or
Jonah when King James VI hired jobbers.

I never mentioned Malcolm X's
(Shakespeare was King James VI)

but ventured a hole for blah
's a norf 'n' sarf. '*BLÁTH,*'

you groaned, '*B-L-Afada-T-H.*
You'll say that *H-A-I-T-C-H.*'

Flower. Ní bás acht á fás.
I stopped once at Béal na mBláth,

where the Big Man fell in the Civil War.
Though the flower fadeth; the 'Mouth of Flowers'.

IV *Confessional*

I have been Enzensberger's
cognitive model, 'a box in
it/labelled Box'; Popa's
'with teeth growing inside of her,
the whole world tiny small';
I have been MacCruiskeen's;
I have been them all.

V *Dimensions*

The walls are Irish, English, Ulster Scots,
Antrim Gaelic; the sky a delta of roots;

the ground vaulted with wings.
The box is a ring:

in this corner a beautiful
woman gone to the devil –

here a lover who newly-dead
with hare's-paws boxed his coffin lid.

The box is a triangle of beams
from the lidless eye;

a slab of flag; a great fulham
flattened by Einstein's discovery.

VI *Smurr*

When the block and tackle shattered
the hoist's canvas sash pulled from an O
into a tear, launching a live mortar. She
wrestled with the sky like a damned angel –
cargo for the Indies the same as glass
or Carrick salt ballast of flesh packed
like a fist. Blame the chandler's cheap rope,
the cheaper owners then watch this smurr
measure the pig's back of Muck Island
as Diarmaid paced out his kill for Finn.
The Gobbins has sobbed blood. Again,
all our children's blood shall wash the land.
If rope-makers are wanton in their art
what of nationbuilders? They think less of us
than of that ass on the dock
where the Norwegian White Gentiles
butchered the Danish Black, less than
that ass of her straw. I can be hanged
for speaking this. Therefore I persevere
and endeavour to form a brotherhood
for Irishmen, their several God
before the grass withereth, the
flower fadeth.

The Name of the Name of the Rose
(for Peter Gomersall)

If you bring roses, don't think you'll move her
by giving the class or variety –
'With Love, these *President Herbert Hoover!'*
or 'O my love is like a hybrid tea...'

Among rose names beauty seldom figures.
A small imagination's beggary
is guilty of *Park Direktor Riggers,*
The Duchess of York, Gertrude Gregory.

We used to drink in 'The Pub With No Name'
until it changed to 'The Duchess of York',
locally pronounced 'The Pub With No Shame'.
No good would come of it. There was soon talk.

They renamed the rose after her divorce,
as if the Duchess or rose cared tuppence.
Since there's no doubt they'll think of something worse
let's suggest *The Arselicker's Comeuppance.*

Poem Ending with a Sausage

Old Svend, so given to apostrophising upon God in the log-book –
a lifelong habit worsened by his tussle with the slyly-coiled line
attached to his first experimental fragmentation harpoon-grenade,
which launched him with it into a school of astonished Pilots
gambolling in the scrotumtightening briny off Finmark in 1864
and his subsequent rescue by a vigilant and agile Basque – prayed
as he was transfixed and preyed upon by an unforeseen problem:

but how he solved it isn't, of course, the subject of this poem
if any, but even if it turned out that it was, bet your fat arse
Mine Poet (as most of his milk-sisters) would make a balls of it,
AND you couldn't trust one of the twisted, two-faced bastards
not to chelp or pun or make some reference to Mr T.S. Eliot,
or suck up to the pro-whale lobby by quoting *Moby Dick* as if
the fish didn't start the trouble when it bit off Ahab's leg,

AND should you ask one of these sea-cabbages what was *the point*
of their ballsed-up two-faced scrimshaw, why it was so *roundabout*
(which is the P.O.S.H. way of asking *WHAT WAS THE BLOODY POINT?*)
why, they look at you like you're shite, sneer about 'metaphor',
whack their flukes about your ears and bugger off through frilly water
like a ballerina with a ladder in her tights God help us all –
take my word: you can't trust a wimp to end with a banger.

The Gloss

Our conquering heroes grasped too late
the stout resistance they had not met,
the fires guiding them to safe harbour
past submarine hulks off Scarborough.
Ashore their winged helmets and dripping furs
stirred folk's envies more often than their fears.
Boys hung on every word they said. A
landlord laid on Karaoke Edda.
Inland, monasteries were signposted
in Esperanto, Geat and Old High Norse,
listing hours monks would be available
for visitors to disembowel.
In time they drove on to the Dales,
their tattoos peeling in the clement gales –
bad ones would blow away both man and horse.
None could hear if they still spoke Old High Norse.
After their first excursion in spring rain
they never saw their testicles again.
They held down their fields with dry stone walls.
The harvest of their fields was dry stone walls.
They carved homes and chesspieces fom these stones
and never lost their hatred of these stones.
All of them were broken by the work.
The berserkers were constantly berserk,
dying so and shipless for their bones
to prop up epitaphs in these stones
with dates wrong and misspellings of their names
moaned the red-haired pedants on pub quiz teams.
The last of these would die in our village,
asked to gloss the Old High Norse for pillage.

NOTES TO THE POEMS

The First Second. My parents inherited a folk-myth that only Jesus Christ grew to six feet exactly. I heard it nowhere else until a few years ago, then from a woman at a Rathcoole writers' group.

Estuary English partly derives from Bill Cosby's 'Ark' routine and Frank Ching's article, which he expanded into the book *Ancestors*.

Fred. See Granzotto's biography *Christopher Columbus*, also Bacchelli's *Why I Never Wrote A Biography of Christopher Columbus*.

Brut. Sir Frederic Madden, K.H., was Keeper of the Manuscripts at the British Museum. His version was published by The Society of Antiquaries, London, 1847.

1992. After losing the world's first copyright war in Ireland, Columba sought exile on the island most simply known in the Old Gaelic as *I* ('island'); as *Hii* in Bede's Anglo-Saxon; *Iou-a* in Pictish, which, mistranscribed, gives us its modern name of Iona.

Note. The Spanish is from St John of the Cross' 'Canción de la llama de amor viva' – 'Song of the Living Flame (not Llama) of Love' – and means 'gentle touch that tastes of eternal life and pays all debt' (*The Penguin Book of Spanish Verse*, ed. Cohen).

The Gift of a Black Egg. Duhig is a Munster Anglicisation of *Ó Dubhthaigh*; *uasal* = noble; *ubh* = egg; *dubh* = black; *Go raibh maith agat* = Thank you; and 'kibosh', whatever some dictionaries might tell you, is from the Irish for 'death-cap' or 'death-hood'.

Traditional. Leeds has more magpies than anywhere else.

The Protestant's Dog-Thieves. Wren Boys nominally toured their locality on St Stephen's Day (Britain's Boxing Day) receiving tributes and leftovers. Often, as in my father's case, this was merely the climax of a year's rural guerilla warfare waged by the disaffected against the respectable. Blueshirts were half-arsed Irish fascists.

If & Ex Libris use material from Malcolm X's autobiography and *Malcolm*, by Bruce Perry. Malcolm said 'books were my university' and liked to speculate on the identity of Shakespeare. Like Jim Harris in Eugene O'Neill's *All God's Chillun Got Wings*, he wanted to be a lawyer. *Na Caca* comes from an Irish epithet for James II of England, Séamus na Caca or James the Shit.

Gyron's Submission. Gyron's is the only part in Alfred Jarry's *Ubu* cycle specified for an actor of colour. Perhaps this was a reference to Nabo, a dwarf from Dahomey rumoured to have been big enough for Louis XIV's Queen.

B I Ballad. British Israelism is found throughout these islands, one of its secret histories. Its imagery is prominent on the banners of the Orange Order, the Royal Arch Purple Chapter and the Royal Black Institution, although most members of these would be embarrassed if asked to confirm its literal truth.

Roll Call. Douglas did indeed stand up to be counted during the making of his film *Spartacus*. He hired 'Sam Jacks' (Dalton Trumbo blacklisted into pseudonyms by McCarthyism) and then posted him for access at the studio gate in his real name, causing a furore.

Portrait of the Art. Danny Kyle, the traditional singer from Glasgow, introduced me to the exploits of 'Double-Jobby' Bobby, whom he worked with in the Clyde yards.

Culchie Gough. Eclipsis is the suppression of the sound of an initial consonant in certain circumstances in Irish (*gCopaleen*).

From the Land of *Uz*. Familiar with 'black' as a term of abuse for Protestants by Catholics, its use by Protestants to abuse the RUC was new to me until this riot.

And in the Depth. Garrett refers to John Holland, inventor of the submarine proper. Holland was formerly with the Christian Brothers, when he introduced the Tonic-Solfa system of musical instruction into Irish schools. Some of his sponsoring Fenians in America became impatient with the slow progress of *The Fenian Ram*, and stole it to exhibit in Madison Square Gardens to raise funds for the 1916 Easter Rising.

Six More Sides to *The Muck Island Box*. The *Box* is a lifebox of Islandmagee's Protestant community by poet Adrian Rice and artist Ross Wilson. They draw on traditions of radical dissenters, 'New Light' Presbyterian philosophers and United Irishmen to analyse other local traditions such as witchcraft and sectarianism. They made Boxes for 100 subscribing friends and neighbours, although some have now been sold on into collections such as those of the Tate Gallery and the Harvard Library. 'The Old Croppy' is no longer visible at Ballycarry Graveyard. *Ní bás acht á fás* ('Not dead but growing') was once a common epitaph. 'Smurr' is a local word meaning a light fall of rain. The ending of this section borrows from the oath of the United Irishmen.